United States Army Shoulder Patches and Related Insignia

By the Author

United States Army Shoulder Patches and Related Insignia From World War I to Korea
1st Division to 40th Division

United States Army Shoulder Patches and Related Insignia From World War I to Korea
41st Division to 106th Division

United States Army Shoulder Patches and Related Insignia

From World War I to Korea

Army Groups, Armies and Corps

William Keller
& Kurt Keller

Schiffer Military History
Atglen, PA

Acknowledgments

Our sincerest gratitude goes out to all that helped and made the production of this volume possible. We wish to thank them for their hospitality and cooperation. It was a unique privilege to be invited to view their collections and photograph the best each had to offer. Without exception, each visit was a wonderful learning experience. Their dedication, not just to collecting, but to the preservation of history, made this project a joy to work on, and the photographs contained within speak volumes to the lifetime commitment it has been for many of them. We are also grateful to the individuals who graciously provided us identification for some of the more unusual pieces. One last note; we would like to especially thank those brave souls who mailed us photos and patches to photograph. Rather than mentioning only those who contributed to this particular volume, all who have contributed to the series will be acknowledged. Special thanks to: Dan Alloggio, Kurt H. Andariese, David S. Angle, Peter M. Bennethum, Gary Castellino, Rocco Collura, Robert A. Erickson, David Fisher, John Foley, Mike Furey, Bob Ford, Scott Glemby, Richard T. Graney, Daniel Griffin, Lt. Col. James E. Mullin (Ret), Charles B. Oellig, Clifford Orth, Bruce J. Pitre, Jr., Gus Radle, James F. Rudy, Garth Thompson, Charles Van Der Eems, John B. Wright, and finally to Randy Hackenburg and Jay Graybeal at the U.S. Army Military History Institute.

To all the soldiers who served, both remembered and forgotten.

Book design by Robert Biondi.
Principal photography by Kurt Keller; additional photography by William Keller.
Dust jacket photo by Robert Biondi.

Library of Congress Catalog Number:2003115389

Printed in China.
ISBN: 0-7643-1921-3

Published by Schiffer Publishing Ltd.
4880 Lower Valley Road
Atglen, PA 19310
Phone: (610) 593-1777
FAX: (610) 593-2002
E-mail: Schifferbk@aol.com.
Visit our web site at: www.schifferbooks.com
Please write for a free catalog.
This book may be purchased from the publisher.
Please include $3.95 postage.
Try your bookstore first.

In Europe, Schiffer books are distributed by:
Bushwood Books
6 Marksbury Ave.
Kew Gardens
Surrey TW9 4JF
England
Phone: 44 (0)208 392-8585
FAX: 44 (0)208 392-9876
E-mail: info@bushwoodbooks.co.uk.
Free postage in the UK. Europe: air mail at cost.
Try your bookstore first.

Contents

Use Guide and Abbreviation Key

Use this section as a quick reference point for the listing and description of each patch. Unlike the first two volumes, each figure now has a heading, and they are as follows:

A = Army
1AAbnA = 1st Allied Airborne Army
AGp = Army Group
C = Corps

Each photo caption contains all the information about each patch: the figure and patch number; the period the patch is from; the country of origin; the specific identification of the patch; and finally the construction description. All patches without a country listed, with the exception of WWI's, are believed to be made in the United States. Information not covered by the introduction will be discussed in the caption when the topic is reached. Please see the sample entries below. For further and more detailed information about period and styles of manufacture please refer to the Introduction section of *United States Army Shoulder Patches and Related Insignia from World War I to Korea (1st Division to 40th Division).*

Fig. A1.61. World War I. 1st Army Signal Corps. Felt on wool.
Translation: 1st Army patch 61, manufactured during the World War I period, 1st Army Signal Corps, felt and wool construction.

Fig. AGp15.3. World War II, England. HE on felt.
Translation: 15th Army Group, patch 3, manufactured during World War II, made in England, hand embroidered on felt.

World War I = 1918 to approximately 1923
Interwar = 1920's to 1941
World War II = 1941 to 1945
Post World War II = 1945 Occupation - early Cold War era
Bullion = Any spun, woven or wrapped metallic thread.

CS = Chain Stitch: 2 top threads attached to base material by a single pick up or backing thread. Under close examination this embroidery type resembles a chain. This technique is usually done with a hand guided embroidery machine. A hand embroidered technique also exists that resembles this stitch pattern.
DI = Distinguished Unit Insignia: Metal insignia with enameled or painted designs commonly found for regimental units. Occasionally these can be found in miniature patch form for wear on overseas caps, lapels and shoulder straps.
ET = Embroidered on Twill: Any patch where exposed twill base material is part of the design of the patch.
FE = Fully Embroidered: The embroidery covers the entire surface of the patch.
Felt = Pressed woolen material that has no weave.
HE = Hand Embroidered: The design of the patch is embroidered with needle and thread by hand.
ME = Machine Embroidered: The design is embroidered on material with a machine guided by a prepared pattern.
ODB = Olive Drab Border
TM = Patch is believed to be theater made but is of an unknown origin.
Wool = Wool that is a woven cloth with or without texture.
? = The possibility exists that the patch is from this period or country of origin.

Introduction

The subject matter of this volume are the patches that were worn by members of Army Groups, Armies, Corps, and the 1st Allied Airborne Army. The patches of some units, such as the Army Groups, have only a few variations pictured. This is mainly due to the fact that they existed for a short period of time and did not have as many personnel assigned to them. Other units, such as the 1st Army, with its greater number of personnel and much longer life span from World War I to this day, has over 100 examples. Overall we were pleased to find at least a few variations for each to give the collector as complete a picture as possible. Altogether this volume shows that the men of these units had as much pride in their patches and creativity as did the soldiers of the Infantry Divisions. The reader may note the book begins with Army patches and not those of the Army Groups. Although an Army Group was organizationally above an Army and as such should be first, the 1st Army was the first American Army organized in the modern era. Additionally, the shear number of Army patches pictured made for a much better beginning. Originally we had planned to release this volume first, however, the amount of material compiled at the time did not allow for it. We will leave it to you to decide which volume you put first on your shelf! We would like to thank again all who helped, in whatever capacity, with the production of this book. With this said, we hope you are just as satisfied with this volume as with the previous ones.

William Keller
Kurt Keller
January 8, 2003

United States Army
Shoulder Patches and Related Insignia

Army Groups, Armies and Corps

Fig. A1.1. World War I. Unidentified Doughboy wearing a ME on felt 1st Army Anti-Aircraft Machine Gun Battalions patch.

Fig. A1.2. World War I. 1st Army Anti-Aircraft Machine Gun Battalions. ME on felt. This patch is the same pattern as the one being worn in Fig. A1.1.

Fig. A1.3. World War I. A medal commemorating the World War I service of Company A, 3rd Anti-Aircraft Machine Gun Battalion with an enameled likeness of the unit patch.

Fig. A1.4. World War I. 1st Army Anti-Aircraft Machine Gun Battalions. Felt on felt with ME winged arrow.

Fig. A1.5. World War I. 1st Army Anti-Aircraft Machine Gun Battalions. ME on wool. This example has the winged arrow descending and does not have the light blue background panel.

Fig. A1.6. World War I. An unidentified Doughboy of the 1st Anti-Aircraft Machine Gun Battalion. Notice the "1" in the top portion of the "A".

Fig. A1.7. World War I. Two unidentified NCOs from a 1st Army Anti-Aircraft Machine Gun Battalion pause to have their picture taken while sight seeing somewhere in Europe.

Fig. A1.8. World War I. An unidentified doughboy from the 3rd Anti-Aircraft Artillery. The "3" in the upper portion and "AA" in the lower portion of the patch are just visible in the photo. It is unclear if he is from an Artillery or Machine Gun unit, as the 1st Army employed both 3 inch guns and 8mm Hotchkiss machine guns in this role.

Fig. A1.9. World War I. Ralph Collier of the 18th Field Artillery Regiment. It is interesting to note that the 18th FA was part of the 3rd Infantry Division, but he is wearing a 1st Army Artillery patch.

Fig. A1.10. World War I. 1st Army Artillery. Felt on wool.

Fig. A1.11. World War I. Harold Ford of the 69th Regiment, Coast Artillery Corps wearing a simple wool 1st Army Artillery patch applied directly to his uniform.

Fig. A1.12. World War I. 1st Army Artillery. ME on felt.

Fig. A1.13. World War I. 1st Army Artillery. ME on wool

Fig. A1.14. World War I. 1st Army Artillery. Felt on felt with ME color section.

Fig. A1.15. World War I. An unidentified engineer wearing a 1st Army Artillery patch. Courtesy of US Army Military History Institute.

Fig. A1.16. World War I. 1st Army Artillery Park. Felt bear on a wool "A" with cotton color section.

Fig. A1.17. World War I. 1st Army Artillery Park. Felt on felt with ME details.

Fig. A1.18. World War I. 1st Army Artillery Park. Felt on wool shoulder patch and a felt on felt miniature Garrison Cap patch.

Fig. A1.19. World War I. 1st Army Railway Artillery Reserve. PFC Lloyd W. Slagle's wool 1st Army patch with bullion lettering and felt oozelfinch.

Fig. A1.20. World War I. 1st Army Railway Artillery Reserve. Felt on wool with separate added HE on wool RAR patch.

Fig. A1.22. World War I. 1st Army Air Service. Wool on wool.

Fig. A1.21. World War I. An unidentified doughboy wearing an unusual 1st Army Air Service patch. The most common variation has a smaller Aero Cockade added to the lower portion of the patch. In this example the cockade is bisected by the cross bar of the "A".

Fig. A1.23. World War I. 1st Army Air Service. Wool on wool.

Fig. A1.24. World War I. 1st Army Air Service. Wool on wool with CS cockade.

Fig. A1.25. World War I. 1st Army Air Service. ME on felt.

Fig. A1.26. World War I. 1st Army Air Service. Liberty Loan.

Fig. A1.27. World War I. An unidentified doughboy wearing the more typical style 1st Army Air Service patch.

Fig. A1.28. World War I. 1st Army Chemical Warfare. Wool "A" with silk color section.

Fig. A1.29. World War I. 1st Army Chemical Warfare, 1st Gas Regiment. All felt construction.

Fig. A1.30. World War I. Unidentified doughboy wearing a 1s Army Engineers patch.

Fig. A1.31. World War I. 1st Army Engineers. All wool construction.

Fig. A1.32. World War I. 1st Army Engineers. Wool tape "A" and wool castle.

Fig. A1.33. World War I. 1st Army Engineers. ME on felt.

Fig. A1.34. World War I. 1st Army Engineers. ME on wool.

Fig. A1.35. World War I. 1st Army Engineers. Liberty Loan.

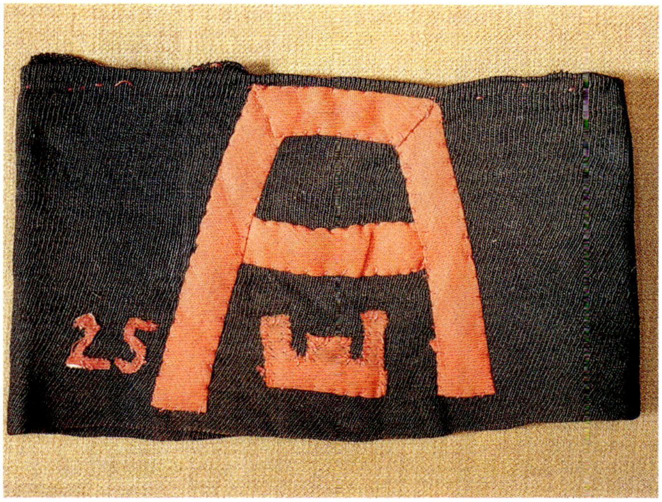

Fig. A1.36. World War I. A brassard from the 25th Engineer Regiment (construction). Linen or cotton applied to a wool armband.

Fig. A1.37. World War I. 40th Engineer Regiment (camouflage). Much like Divisional insignia with added miniature Army of Occupation patches, 1st Army patches were worn in conjunction with additional unit patches. Sometimes referred to as a salamander, the figure represents a chameleon, an animal which can change color to match its surroundings. Wool 1st Army with a felt castle and a wool chameleon on a felt background.

Fig. A1.38. World War I. 56th Engineer Regiment (searchlight). Wool 1st Army with a felt castle and a wool on wool 56th Engineer with HE details.

Fig. A1.39. World War I. Detail of a 56th Engineer Regiment (searchlight) pennant.

Fig. A1.40. World War I. 56th Engineer Regiment (searchlight). Wool 1st Army with felt "SL" and castle.

Fig. A1.41. World War I. 1st Army Headquarters. All wool construction.

Fig. A1.42. World War I. 1st Army Medical Corps. Felt on a wool background.

Fig. A1.43. World War I. 1st Army Medical Corps. Wool 1st Army with cloth tape color section.

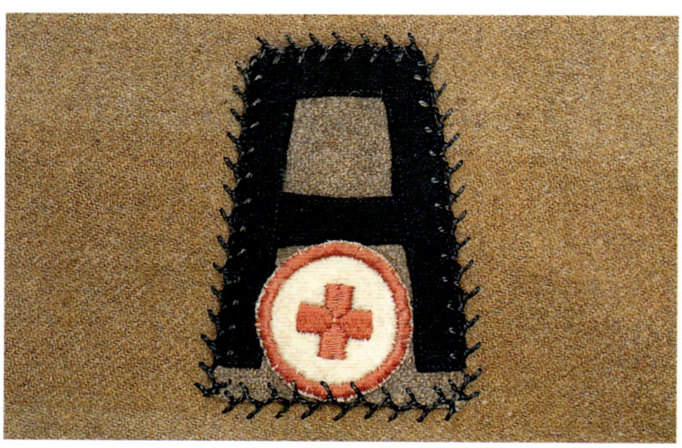

Fig. A1.44. World War I. 1st Army Medical Corps. Felt on wool with added ME on felt medical insignia.

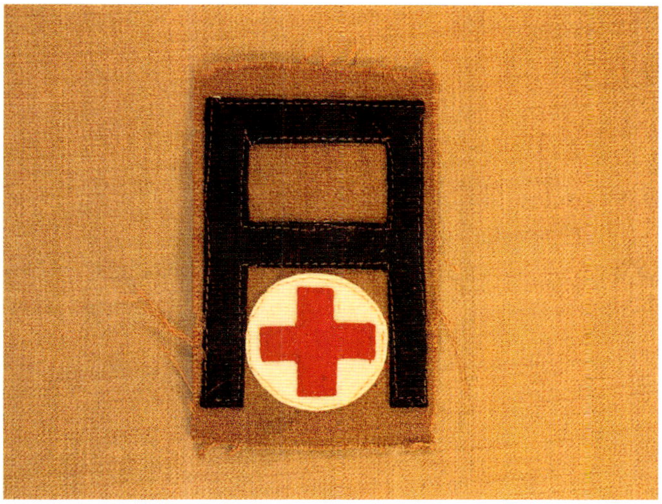

Fig. A1.45. World War I. 1st Army Medical Corps. All felt on a wool background.

Fig. A1.46. World War I. 1st Army Military Police. Wool on wool with bullion and wool color section.

Fig. A1.47. World War I. Two unidentified doughboys from the 1st Army Motor Transportation Corps.

Fig. A1.48. World War I. 1st Army Motor Transportation Corps. Wool 1st Army with wool color section.

Fig. A1.49. World War I. Doughboys aboard ship, two of which are wearing 1st Army Motor Transportation Corps patches.

Fig. A1.50. World War I. 1st Army Motor Transportation Corps. All wool construction. This variation features the "MTC" monogram.

Fig. A1.51. World War I. 1st Army Motor Transportation Corps. ME on felt.

Fig. A1.52. World War I. 1st Army Ordnance. All wool construction. This patch was worn by Marshall Nye of the 4th Heavy Mobile Ordnance Repair Shop.

Fig. A1.53. World War I. 1st Army Ordnance. Wool on wool with HE flaming bomb.

Figs. A1.54 and A1.55. World War I. 1st Army Ordnance. All wool construction. The significance of the artillery shell is unknown.

Fig. A1.56. World War I. 1st Army, 4th Heavy Mobile Ordnance Repair Shop. ME on wool.

Fig. A1.57. World War I. 1st Army, 8th Heavy Mobile Ordnance Repair Shop. All wool construction.

Fig. A1.58. World War I. 1st Army Ordnance, unknown unit. All felt construction.

Fig. A1.59. World War I. 1st Army Quartermaster Corps. ME on wool.

Fig. A1.60. World War I. 1st Army Quartermaster Corps. Wool on wool with hand embroidered quartermaster insignia.

Fig. A1.61. World War I. 1st Army Signal Corps. Felt on wool.

Figs. A1.62 and A1.63. World War I. 1st Army Signal Corps. Felt on wool with ME signal flags.

Fig. A1.64. World War I. 1st Army Signal Corps. This unusual patch combination was worn by a member of Pigeon Company 1, 9th Field Signal Battalion of the 5th Infantry Division. Wool on wool 1st Army with added ME on felt signal flags and a bullion on wool pigeon.

Fig. A1.65. World War I. An unidentified doughboy wearing a combination 1st Army patch. The top portion has a 37th Infantry Division insignia, and the bottom portion a 5th Corps insignia. The 37th Division was part of the 5th Corps during the Meuse-Argonne Operation of September 21, 1918, to November 11, 1918. During the same period the 5th Corps was part of the 1st Army.

Fig. A1.66. World War I. 1st Army, 5th Corps, 37th Division. ME on felt. This is the same style patch being worn in Fig. A1.65.

Fig. A1.67. World War I. 1st Army, 1st Corps. Wool on wool construction.

Fig. A1.68. World War I. 1st Army, 28th Division. Felt on wool.

Fig. A1.69. World War I. 1st Army, 28th Division. Felt "A" with a wool 28th Division, all on a wool background.

Fig. A1.70. World War I. 1st Army, 41st Division. This patch was worn by a member of the 1st North Dakota National Guard Infantry Regiment, which was redesignated the 164th Infantry Regiment on September 19, 1917, after being inducted into federal service. It is unknown if this combination was specific to the 164th or was employed by other units within the 41st Division. Wool 1st Army with a wool and bullion 41st Division.

Fig. A1.71. World War I. 1st Army, 41st Division. Felt 1st Army with a Liberty Loan 41st Division.

Fig. A1.72. World War I. 1st Army, Advance Section, Service of Supply. ME on wool.

Fig. A1.73. World War I. W.J.B. Humphries of Company E, 3rd Pioneer Infantry Regiment. Notice the horizontal artillery shell patch beneath the 1st Army and the "US 3" collar disk. It should be noted the possibility exists that other Pioneer Regiments assigned to the 1st Army also used this same patch configuration. However, all examples encountered and pictured are attributed to the 3rd.

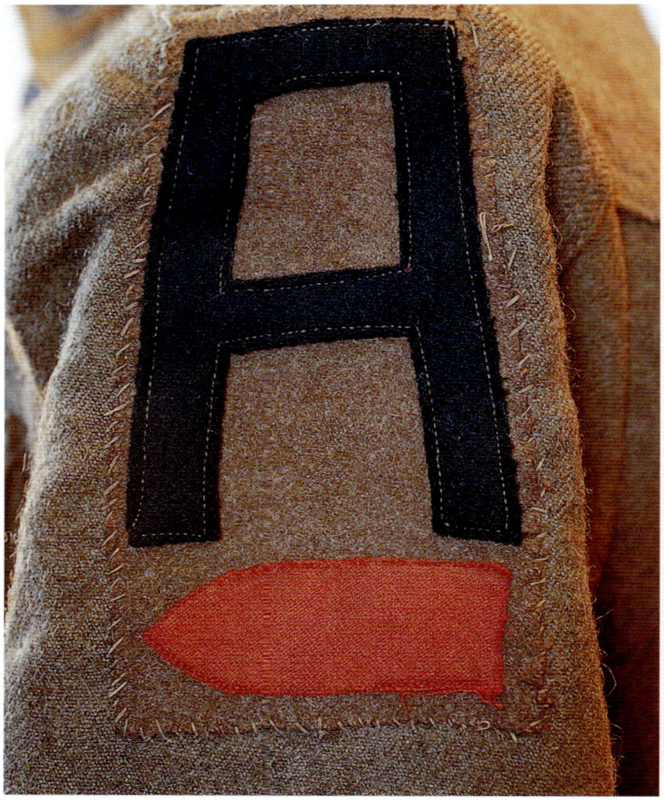

Fig. A1.74. World War I. 1st Army, 3rd Pioneer Infantry Regiment. All wool construction.

Fig. A1.75. World War I. 1st Army, 3rd Pioneer Infantry Regiment. ME on felt.

Fig. A1.78. World War I. 1st Army Ammunition Train. Wool 1st Army with felt color section.

Fig. A1.79. World War I. 1st Army, 59th Ammunition Train. Felt on wool.

Fig. A1.77. World War I. 1st Army, 3rd Pioneer Infantry Regiment. Pfc. Olson's ME on felt patch on his cotton tunic. This patch is the same style as in Fig. A1.75 but with the background material removed.

Fig. A1.76. World War I. Pfc. Charles W. Olson of Company A, 3rd Pioneer Infantry Regiment. Although his 1st Army patch lacks the horizontal artillery shell, the "US 3" collar disk is evident.

Fig. A1.80. World War I. 1st Army, unknown unit. Wool 1st Army with HE on wool "E". It is possible the "E" is for Artillery Excellence, an award given by the Coast Artillery Corps to batteries for an excellent rating in target practice. Many CAC units operated in the 1st Army and one of them may have chosen this as their insignia.

Fig. A1.81. World War I. 1st Army, unknown unit. The 147th Field Artillery Regiment utilized a skull and cross bones as their insignia and operated under the 1st Army. However, it is unknown if this is a patch for that unit. Felt 1st Army with hand, embroidered skull, and cross bones.

Fig. A1.82. World War I. 1st Army, unknown unit. ME on felt. The upper portion of the color section is white and the lower portion is faded orange.

Fig. A1.83. World War I. 1st Army, unknown unit. ME on wool.

Fig. A1.84. World War II. An unidentified 1st Army Engineer. During the Interwar period the 1st Army adopted a new color identification system for units with the 1st. Unlike World War I, the color designating a specific branch of service was in the upper portion of the "A". The color of the panel was made to coincide with the piping on the garrison cap. The system also replaced the numerous symbols employed during the Great War. For example, the engineer castle was replaced by a red panel bordered in white.

Fig. A1.85. Interwar. 1st Army Armor. ME on wool.

Fig. A1.86. Interwar. 1st Army Artillery. Felt on felt. This example was made in the World War I style, probably before the top panel change over occurred.

Fig. A1.88. Interwar. 1st Army Artillery. Felt on World War I officer's whipcord material. Courtesy of US Army Military History Institute.

Fig. A1.87. Interwar. 1st Army Artillery. All felt. Courtesy of US Army Military History Institute.

Fig. A1.89. Interwar. 1st Army Artillery. Felt on officer's dark OD wool elastique. Courtesy of US Army Military History Institute.

Fig. A1.90. Interwar. 1st Army Artillery. ME of officer's dark OD wool elastique.

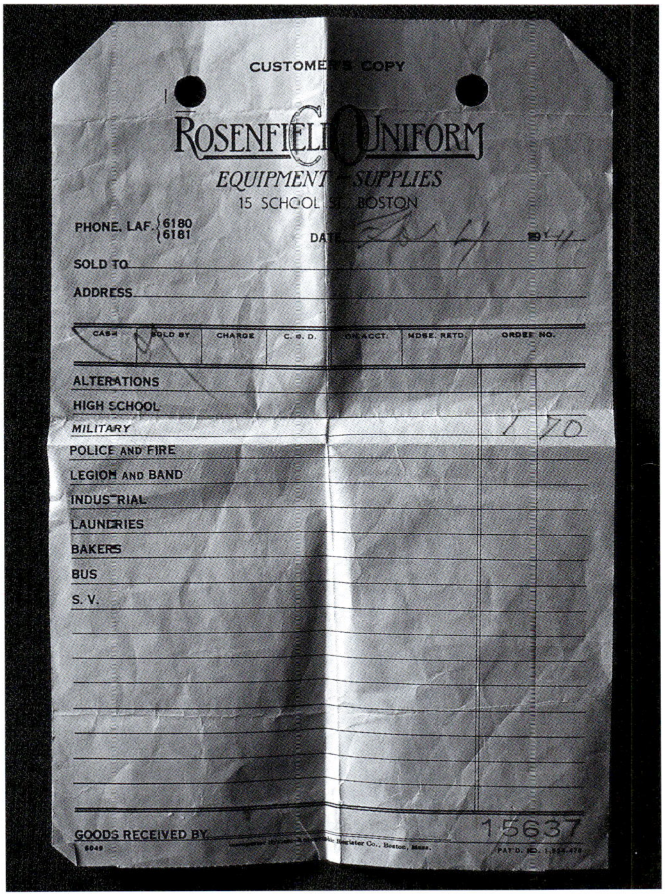

CUSTOMER'S COPY

ROSENFIELD UNIFORM CO

EQUIPMENT — SUPPLIES

15 SCHOOL ST. BOSTON

PHONE. LAF. 6180 / 6181

DATE 19

SOLD TO

ADDRESS

CASH	SOLD BY	CHARGE	C. O. D.	ON ACCT.	MDSE. RETD.	ORDER NO.

ALTERATIONS

HIGH SCHOOL

MILITARY

POLICE AND FIRE

LEGION AND BAND

INDUSTRIAL

LAUNDRIES

BAKERS

BUS

S. V.

GOODS RECEIVED BY

15637

Fig. A1.93. Interwar. Receipt from the Rosenfeld Uniform Company of Boston, dated February 4, 1941, for the patches in Figs. A1.91 and A1.92.

Figs. A1.91 and A1.92. Interwar. 1st Army Artillery. ME on felt with felt color panel.

Fig. A1.94. World War II. 1st Army Artillery. FE patch with added satin panel.

Fig. A1.95. Post World War II, Germany. 1st Army Artillery. Cotton embroidered to a wool base.

Fig. A1.96. World War II/Post World War II. 1st Army Artillery. US made FE patch with added cotton color panel and hand embroidered border. This patch was worn by a member of the 116th Antiaircraft Artillery Gun Battalion.

Fig. A1.97. World War II/Post World War II. 1st Army Artillery. US made FE patch with added hand embroidered color panel and border.

Fig. A1.98. Post World War II, Germany. 1st Army Artillery. Cotton tape on a wool background with ME border. This patch was worn by a member of the 126th Antiaircraft Artillery Gun Battalion.

Fig. A1.99. Post World War II, Germany. 1st Army Artillery. HE on wool.

Fig. A1.100. Interwar. 1st Army Aviation. ME on wool.

Fig. A1.101. Interwar/World War II. 1st Army Aviation. FE.

Fig. A1.102. Interwar. 1st Army Aviation. Felt on officer's dark CD wool elastique. It is believed that this patch is for aviation. Under close examination the hue of the red is a red-orange. The black may have been substituted for ultramarine blue for ease of manufacture.

Fig. A1.103. Interwar. 1st Army Cavalry. All felt construction.

Fig. A1.104. Interwar. 1st Army Chemical Warfare. Felt on tropical worsted wool.

Fig. A1.105. Interwar. 1st Army Chemical Warfare. ME on wool.

Fig. A1.106. Interwar/World War II. 1st Army Chemical Warfare. FE.

Fig. A1.107. Interwar. 1st Army Detached Enlisted Men's List. ME on wool. The D.E.M.L. were a variety of 1st Army enlisted personnel, such as prison guards and recruiters.

Fig. A1.108. Interwar/World War II. 1st Army Detached Enlisted Men's List. FE.

Fig. A1.109. World War II/Post World War II. 1st Army Engineers. US made FE with added CS color panel.

Fig. A1.110. Post World War II, Germany. 1st Army Engineers. HE on wool with ME border.

Fig. A1.111. Post World War II, Germany. 1st Army Engineers. Cotton cloth ME to a wool background with a CS color panel.

Fig. A1.112. Interwar. 1st Army Infantry. Felt on wool.

Fig. A1.113. Interwar. 1st Army Infantry. ME on wool.

Fig. A1.114. Interwar. 1st Army Medical. ME on wool.

Fig. A1.115. Interwar. 1st Army Medical. ME on wool.

Fig. A1.116. Interwar/World War II. 1st Army Medical. FE.

Fig. A1.117. Interwar. 1st Army Military Police. Felt on twill.

Fig. A1.118. Interwar. 1st Army Military Police. ME on wool.

Fig. A1.119. Interwar/World War II. 1st Army Military Police. FE.

Fig. A1.120. Interwar/World War II. 1st Army Ordnance. FE.

Fig. A1.121. World War II/Post World War II. 1st Army Crdnance. US made FE patch with HE color sections.

Fig. A1 122. Interwar. 1st Army Quartermaster. Felt on wool.

Fig. A1.123. Interwar. 1st Army Quartermaster. ME on wool.

Figs. A1.125 and A1.126. Interwar/World War II. 1st Army Signal Corps. FE.

Fig. A1.124. Interwar/World War II. 1st Army Quartermaster. FE.

Fig. A1.127. Post World War II, Germany. 1st Army Signal Corps. HE on cotton with felt color panel.

Figs. A1.128 and A1.129. Interwar. 1st Army Finance Department. FE.

Fig. A1.130. World War II. Major General Gerow, commander of the 5th Corps, congratulates Lieutenant Colonel Carl I. Isley on winning the Distinguished Service Cross for bravery under fire in France, September 11, 1944. U.S. Army Signal Corps. During World War I and the Interwar period 1st Army patches with no symbols or color sections were intended for Headquarters personnel. Shortly after America's entrance into World War II the unadorned designed was adopted for wear by all members of the 1st Army.

Fig. A1.131. Interwar. 1st Army Headquarters. Felt on wool.

Fig. A1.132. Interwar. 1st Army Headquarters. ME on felt.

Fig. A1.133. World War II, England. FE.

Fig. A1.134. World War II, England. Silk screened on oil cloth.

Figs. A1.135 and A1.136. World War II. ME on twill.

Fig. A1.137. Post World War II, Germany. FE.

Fig. A1.138. Post World War II, Germany. HE.

Fig. A1.139. Post World War II, Japan. FE.

Fig. A1.140. Post World War II, Japan. FE. Shortly after World War II the design of the 1st Army patch was changed to a white and red scheme. The example on the left shows the proper configuration, and the example on the right is an error with the colors reversed.

Fig. A1.141. Post World War II, Japan. Bullion and felt construction. Courtesy of US Army Military History Institute.

Fig. A1.142. Post World War II, Japan. HE with bullion and quilted background. This patch is still in its original cellophane wrapper.

Fig. A2.1. World War I Unidentified 2nd Army doughboy.

Fig. A2.5. World War I. Liberty Loan.

Figs. A2.2 to A2.4. World War I. HE on wool.

Fig. A2.6. World War I. Unidentified PFC from Company G, 112th Infantry Regiment (28th Division).

Fig. A2.7. World War I. 2nd A-my Air Service. All wool patch with added HE on wool Air Service Cockade.

Fig. A2.8. World War I. 2nd Army Air Service. All wool construction.

Fig. A2.9. World War I. 2nd Arny Engineers. ME on wool.

Fig. A2.10. World War I. 2nd Army Air Service. Wool patch with added felt Air Service Cockade. The alternate design for the 2nd Army in the Great War was an upper case "B".

Fig. A2.11. World War I. Alternate design 2nd Army Engineers. Felt on wool with HE castle.

Fig. A2.12. World War I. Alternate design 2nd Army, 4th Corps. Liberty Loan.

Fig. A2.14. Interwar/World War II. ME on felt.

Fig. A2.13. Interwar. ME on wool.

Figs. A2.15 and A2.16. World War II. ME on khaki twill.

Fig. A2.17. World War II. ME on olive drab twill.

Fig. A2.18. World War II. ME on herring bone twill.

Fig. A2.19. World War II. FE. Square corner variation.

Fig. A3.1. World War I. Two unidentified Artillery Lieutenants from the 3rd Army. The 3rd United States Army was not formally organized until November 15, 1918, and as such never took place in any combat operations. It was, however, employed as the American element of the Allied Army of Occupation in the Rhineland area of Germany. This is why in period references it is sometimes called the Army of Occupation. The design of the patch reflects this with white "A" and red "O".

Fig. A3.2. World War I. HE on felt .

Fig. A3.3. World War I. HE on wool. The embroidered dashed outline was used as a guide when cutting a single patch from a larger sheet of patches.

Fig. A3.4. World War I. Wool on felt with HE "A". Courtesy of US Army Military History Institute.

Fig. A3.5. World War I. A group of doughboys from a 3rd Army Motor Transportation unit passing the time.

Fig. A3.6. World War I. CS on wool.

Fig. A3.7. World War I. CS on satin with a cord border.

Fig. A3.8. World War I. Soutache "A" and CS border on wool.

Fig. A3.9. World War I. Soutache "A" and ribbed tape border on felt.

Fig. A3.10. World War I. Unidentified 3rd Army Infantryman. Of note are the blue felt backing circles behind his collar disks.

Fig. A3.11. World War I. ME on felt.

Fig. A3.12. World War I. Liberty Loan.

Fig. A3.13. World War I . HE on wool with bullion "A".

Fig. A3.14. World War I. Cotton field with HE border, bullion "A" and detail on a wool base.

Fig. A3.15. World War I. Miniature Army of Occupation patches. Left: ME on felt. Right: Ribbed tape on wool. Miniatures like these were often applied directly to division or corps patches to show 3rd Army service.

Figs. A3.16 and A3.17. World War I. Miniature Army of Occupation patch. All felt. In cases where placement of a miniature 3rd Army patch would obscure details or the design of a soldier's unit patch, it was sometimes placed beneath it. Occasionally, as with these two examples, it was sewn above the service chevrons. Both of these examples are on 89th Division uniforms.

Fig. A3.18. World War I. Pictured here is Caryl Holden. He is wearing an interesting version of a 3rd Army patch believed to be for 3rd Army Train units. Notice the "T" superimposed over the "A". The only two listings for non-divisional 3rd Army Train units were the 3rd Army Sanitation Train and the 3rd Army Provisional Supply Train.

Fig. A3.19. World War I. 3rd Army, 32nd Division. ME on felt.

Fig. A3.20. 3rd Army Air Service. Liberty Loan. The alternate design for the 3rd Army in World War 1 was a capital "C".

Fig. A3.23. Interwar. ME on officer's dark OD wool elastique.

Figs. A3.21 and A3.22. Interwar. ME on wool.

Fig. A3.24. World War II. ME on twill.

Fig. A3.25. World War II. FE, ODB.

Fig. A3.26. World War II, England. FE, ODB.

Fig. A3.27. World War II. FE. Wide border variation.

Fig. A3.28. Post World War II. Major General William C. Case points out the 3rd Army insignia on a Military Police Jeep. Courtesy of US Army Military History Institute.

Fig. A3.29. Post World War II, TM. HE on felt with bullion "A" and detail.

Fig. A3.30. Post World War II, Germany. HE on felt with bullion "A".

Fig. A3.31. Post World War II, Germany. HE on felt with bullion "A" and border.

Fig. A3.32. Post World War II, Germany. Bullion "A" and red bullion border on felt.

Fig. A3.33. Post World War II. US made FE patch with German made HE on felt nickname tab. During the fighting in Europe the 3rd Army was commanded by George S. Patton, and "Blood and Guts" was General Patton's nickname.

Fig. A4.1. Interwar. Felt on felt.

Fig. A4.4. World War II. FE, ODB.

Figs. A4.2 and A4.3. Interwar/World War II. ME on felt. The stems of the four leaf clovers in these two examples point in opposite directions.

Figs. A4.5 and A4.6. World War II. FE. Notice again the different directions of the stems.

Fig. A4.7. World War II/Post World War II, TM?. This nice example with a checker board effect to the bullion may be US made. Bullion clover with HE border on a felt background.

Fig. A4.8. Post World War II, Korea. Bullion on wool.

Fig. A5.1. World War II. FE.

Fig. A5.2. World War II, Italy. Woven.

Fig. A5.3. World War II, Italy. HE on satin.

Fig. A5.5. World War II, Italy. CS on satin.

Fig. A5.4. World War II, Italy. CS on wool.

Fig. A5.6. World War II, Italy. HE on a satin background all on a wool base.

Fig. A5.7. World War II, Italy. HE on satin with bullion detail on a felt base.

Fig. A5.8. World War II, TM?. Bullion on felt with a wool border.

Fig. A5.9. World War II, Italy. Bullion on wool.

Fig. A5.10. World War II, Italy. Bullion on wool with a bullion border all on a wool base.

Figs. A5.11 and A5.12. World War II, Italy. Bullion on felt with bullion border all on a felt base.

Fig. A5.13. World War II, Italy. Bullion on satin with a HE border all on a felt base.

Fig. A5.14. World War II, Italy. Bullion on velvet.

Fig. A5.15. Post World War II, Germany. FE.

Fig. A5.16. Post World War II, Germany. Bullion and cotton cording on felt with a cord border on a twill base.

Fig. A5.17. Post World War II, Japan. FE.

Fig. A5.18. World War II. US made FE patch with a ME on satin Italian made tab.

Fig. A5.19. Post World War II. FE patch and tab.

Fig. A5.20. World War II, Italy. Miniature garrison cap patch. HE on satin on a twill base.

Fig. A5.21. Post World War II. 5th Army shooting competition patch. FE.

Fig. A5.22. World War II, Italy. 5th Army Christmas card.

Fig. A5.23. World War II, Italy. Souvenir 5th Army pin.

Fig. A5.24. World War II, Italy. Miniature patch type DI. Painted brass with spring pin closure.

Fig. A6.1. From left to right: Major General, William O. Reeder, Deputy Chief Signal Officer, Washington D.C.; Colonel Lloyd C. Parsons, Signal Officer 6th Army and Colonel Frederick H. L. Ryder, Chief of Staff, Southern Military District at a reserve officer's meeting held in the State Building, Los Angles District. Major General Reeder is wearing a theater made CBI patch, and the colonels are wearing US made FE patches. Courtesy of US Army Military History Institute.

Fig. A6.2. World War II. US made FE patch with added bullion.

Fig. A6.5. Post World War II, Japan. HE silk and bullion cording on Japanese officer's uniform wool.

Figs. A6.3 and A6.4. Post World War II, Japan. HE silk.

Fig. A6.6. Post World War II, Japan. HE bullion and silk.

Fig. A6.7. Post World War II, Germany. HE on felt.

Fig. A6.8. Post World War II, Germany. Red bullion on felt all on a cotton base. Courtesy of US Army Military History Institute.

Fig. A7.1. World War II. Lieutenant General Alexander M. Patch, Jr., Commanding General of the 7th Army, talks with Sergeant Dan J. Boyd somewhere in France, December 30, 1944. General Patch is wearing a US made FE shoulder patch. U.S. Army Signal Corps.

Figs. A7.2 and A7.3. World War II, Italy. HE on satin.

Fig. A7.4. World War II/Post World War II, France. FE.

Fig. A7.5. Post World War II, Germany. A pair of uncut woven patches. These examples illustrate how this style of patch was manufactured, back to back on a long roll of material.

Fig. A7.6. Post World War II, Germany. FE yellow border variation.

Fig. A7.7. Post World War II, Germany. HE on felt.

Fig. A7.8. Post World War II, Germany. HE on felt with cello cord border.

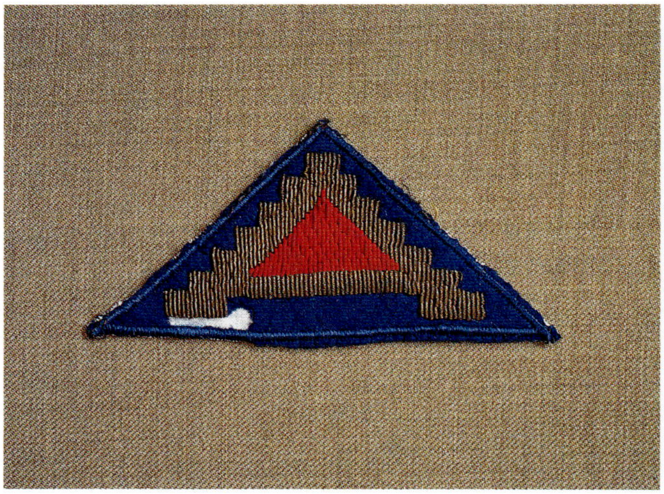

Fig. A7.9. Post World War II, Germany. Gold and red bullion on felt with a machine embroidered edge.

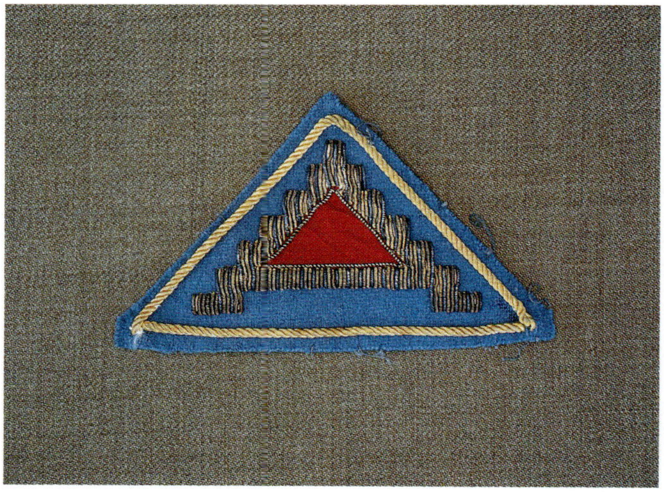

Fig. A7.10. Post World War II. TM. Bullion on wool with cord border.

Fig. A7.11. Post World War II, Germany. Bullion on felt with bullion cord edge.

Fig. A7.12. Post World War II, Germany. Bullion on felt with bullion tape border.

Fig. A7.13. Post World War II, Japan. Silk embroidery on a silk background with bullion details.

Fig. A7.14. Post World War II, Germany. Machine embroidered bulli‹n on felt with integral nickname tab.

Fig. A7.15. Post World War II, Germany. Bullion on felt patch and nickname tab.

Fig. A7.16. Post World War II, German‹. Bullion on felt with integral ›ickname tab and bullion cord edge.

Fig. A7.17. Post World War II, Germany. Bullion on felt with ntegral nickname tab and bullion cord edge.

Fig. A7.18. Post World War II. A com›arison two different FE nick›ame tabs. US made, top and German made, bot‹om.

Fig. A7.19. Post World War II, Germany. Bullion on felt w th cello cord edge nicknamc tab. This example has the number 7 in place of t›e word.

Fig. A8.1. Post Wor d War II. General Maxwell D. Taylor, Commanding Officer of the 8th Army, seen here greeting fellow officers. The general is wear ng a theater made patch. Courtesy of US Army Military History Institute.

Fig. A8.2. Post World War II, Japan. FE silk.

Fig. A8.3. Post World War II, Japan. FE. Though not a common form, the character at the center of the patch when translated reads "Korea".

Fig. A8.4. Post World War II, Japan. HE on silk.

Fig. A8.5. Post World War II, Korea. HE on twill.

Fig. A8.6. Post World War II, Korea. FE on wool.

Fig. A8.7. Post World War II, Japan. Bullion on felt.

Fig. A8.8. Post World War II, Japan. Bullion on wool with a ME border.

Fig. A8.12. Post World War II, Japan. Bullion on wool with bullion border.

Fig. A8.13. Post World War II, Japan. Bullion on silk with bullion border.

Figs. A8.14 and A8.15. Post World War II, Japan. Bullion on silk quilted background with bullion border.

Figs. A8.9 to A8.11. (*Above and following*) Post World War II, Japan. Bullion on felt with bullion border.

Fig. A8.16. Post World War II. US made FE patch with Japanese made ME on silk tab.

Fig. A8.17. Post World War II, Korea. 8th Army Depot Command. ME on twill integral patch and tab.

Fig. A8.18. Post World War II, Korea. 8th Army Non-Commissioned Officer Academy. FE.

Fig. A8.19. Post World war II, Korea. 8th Army Northern Area Command. FE.

Fig. A8.20. Post World War II, Korea 8th Army Support Command. ME on twill integral patch and tabs.

Fig. A8.21. Post World War II, Korea. 8th Army Support Command. ME on satin integral patch and tab.

Fig. A8.22. Post World War II, Korea. 8th Army Support Command. FE on twill integral patch and tabs.

Fig. A8.23. Post World War II, Japan. 8th Army Support Command. Bullion on felt patch with integral tab.

Fig. A8.24. Post World War II, Japan. Bullion on felt patch and tab.

Fig. A8.25. Post World War II, Korea. Bullion on wool patch and tab.

Fig. A8.26. Post World War II, Korea. Bullion on wool integral patch and tab.

Fig. A8.27. Post World War II, Japan. Bullion on felt integral patch and tabs. The numbers on the lower tab refer to the years 1964 through 1966.

Fig. A8.28. Post World War II, Japan. 8th Army Pistol Team jacket patch. FE.

Fig. A8.29. Post World War II, Japan. 8th Army Rifle Team jacket patch. FE.

Fig. A8.30. Post World War II, Japan. 8th Army Automatic Rifle Team jacket patch. FE.

Fig. A8.31. Post World War II, Korea. 1957 shooting tournament jacket patch. ME on satin and twill.

Fig. A8.32. Post World War II, Japan. 8th Army souvenir scarf. HE silk and bullion on silk.

Fig. A8.33. Post World War II, Japan. 8th Army novelty patch. "Chairborne" was a tongue-in-cheek take off on an Airborne tab and used by clerical and support personnel with desk jobs. Hence the typewriter, pens, and swivel chair. Bullion on a quilted silk background with a bullion border.

Fig. A9.1. World War II. PFC. Albert Memory, Jr., inspects a M-20 Armored Car which ran over three Teller mines on the road leading into Albaxen, Germany, the last town to be taken by the 9th Army before the Weser River. U.S. Army Signal Corps.

Fig. A9.2. World War II/Post World War II, TM. CS on cotton. This patch could be made in either Belgium or Germany.

Fig. A9.3. Post World War II, Germany. FE.

Fig. A9.4. Post World War II, Germany. ME on felt.

Fig. A9.5. Post World War II, Korea. ME on satin.

Fig. A9.6. Post World War II. US made FE patch with German added bullion.

Fig. A9.7. Post World War II, Germany. Bullion on wool.

Fig. A9.8. Post World War II, Germany. Bullion on felt.

Fig. A9.9. Post World War II, Germany. Bullion on felt.

Fig. A9.10. Post World War II. US made FE patch with a TM tab embroidered to an Ike jacket.

Fig. A10.1. World War II. FE.

Fig. A10.2. Post World War II, Germany. HE on felt with bullion detail.

Fig. A15.1. World War II. An unidentified 15th Army MP.

Fig. A15.2. World War II. FE.

Figs. A15.3. Post World War II, Germany. HE on twill.

Fig. A15.4. Post World War II, Germany. HE on felt with bullion border.

Fig. 1AAbnA.1. World War II. Lieutenant General Lewis H. Brereton, Commanding General of the 1st Allied Airborne Army, giving a speech at a ceremony where Air Vice Marshal L. N. Hollinghurst received the Distinguish Flying Cross. U.S. Army Signal Corps.

Fig. 1AAbnA.2. World War II. Comparison of two different US made FE patches.

Fig. 1AAbnA.3. World War II, England. ME on felt.

Fig. 1AAbnA.4. World War II, England. Side by side comparison of two different ME on wool variations. These variations feature a separate Allied Airborne tab which is attached to the patch by the line of embroidery at the top.

Fig. 1AAbnA.5. World War II, England. HE on wool.

Fig. 1AAbnA.6. Post World War II, Germany. Bullion on felt with bullion border.

Figs. 1AAbnA.7 and 1AAbnA.8. World War II/Post World War II, TM. FE. There are a number of variations that omit the word "Allied". The significance of this is unknown; however, it is possible this was done to mirror the black airborne tab worn by the 17th and 101st Airborne Divisions, which both operated under the Army.

Fig. 1AAbnA.9 and 1AAbnA.10. World War II/Post World War II, TM. FE.

Fig. 1AAbnA.11. World War II/Post World War II, TM. ME on twill with bullion border.

Fig. 1AAbnA.12. Post World War II, Germany. HE cording on twill.

Fig. 1AAbnA.13. Post World War II, Germany. Bullion and cello cording on wool with HE color section.

Fig. 1AAbnA.14. Post World War II, Germany. Bullion and cello cording on felt with HE color section attached to a wool base.

Figs. 1AAbnA.15. Post World War II, Germany. Bullion on felt with HE color section and black cord border.

Fig. 1AAbnA.16. Post World War II, Germany. Bullion on felt and HE color section with a cello border.

Fig. 1AAbnA.17. Post World War II, Germany. Bullion on wool.

Fig. AGp1.1. World War II. FE

Fig. AGp1.2. World War II. FE. Red "I" variation.

Fig. AGp1.3. World War II, England. ME on wool. Courtesy of the US Army Military History Institute.

Fig. AGp6.1. World War II. An unidentified Major who served with the 6th Army Group receiving a bronze star.

Fig. AGp6.2. World War II. Comparison of two US made FE patches.

Fig. AGp6.3. World War II, England. ME on wool.

Fig. AGp6.4. World War II. Lieutenant Colonel Henry Cabbot Lodge, Jr., 6th Army Group Chief Liaison Officer, talks to Sergeant George Russell of Company C, 411th Infantry Regiment, 103rd Division at a mortar position overlooking the German held town of Rothbach, France, March 6, 1945. U.S. Army Signal Corps.

Fig. AGp12.1. World War II. Brigadier General Lewis, Deputy Chief of Staff, 12th Army Group, greets members of the Senate Military Affairs Committee on their arrival at Eagle Air Strip, Wiesbaden, Germany, on June 1, 1945. U.S. Army Signal Corps.

Fig. AGp12.2. World War II. FE.

Fig. AGp12.3. Post World War II, TM. ME on wool.

Fig. AGp12.4. Post World War II, TM. ME on twill.

Fig. AGp12.5. Post World War II, TM. ME on satin.

Fig. AGp12.6. Post World War II, TM. CS on twill.

Fig. AGp12.7. Post World War II, TM. Twill with cotton tape stripe and ME border.

Fig. AGp12.8. Post World War II, TM. All felt construction.

Figs. AGp15.1 and AGp15.2. World War II. US made FE.

Fig. AGp15.3. World War II, England. HE on felt.

Fig. AGp15.4. World War II, England. Printed design on oil cloth.

Fig. C1.1. World War I. Unidentified doughboy of the Quartermaster Corps wearing a 1st Corps patch.

Fig. C1.2. World War I. ME or felt.

Fig. C1.4. Interwar. Felt on wool.

Fig. C1.3. World War I. Unidentified Lieutenant Bandsman wearing a ME on felt or wool 1st Corps patch.

Fig. C1.5. Interwar. Felt on felt.

Fig. C1.6. Interwar. ME on wool.

Figs. C1.7 and C1.8. World War II. FE, ODB.

Fig. C1.9. Post World War II, Japan. Fully hand embroidered silk. Courtesy of US Army Military History Institute.

Fig. C1.10. Post World War II, Japan. HE silk wool.

Figs. C1.11 and C1.12. Post World War II, Japan. Bullion on wool.

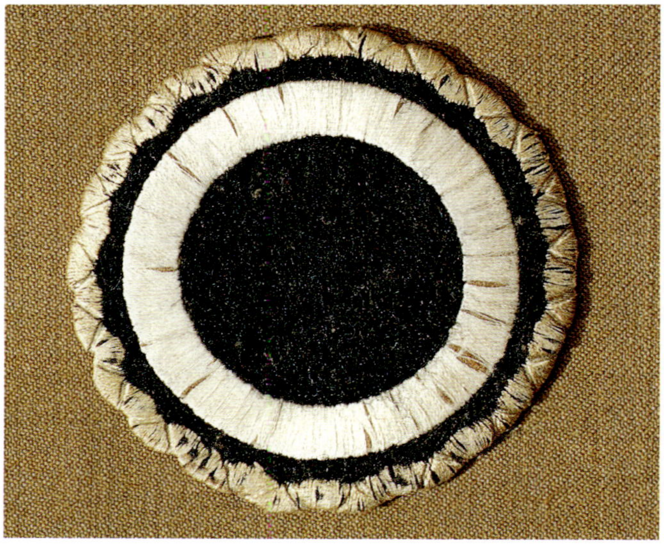

Figs. C1.13 and C1.14. Post World War II, Korea. ME on wool.

Fig. C1.15. Post World War II, Korea. ME on satin.

Fig. C1.16. Post World War II, Korea. Satin ascots with miniature ME on twill patches.

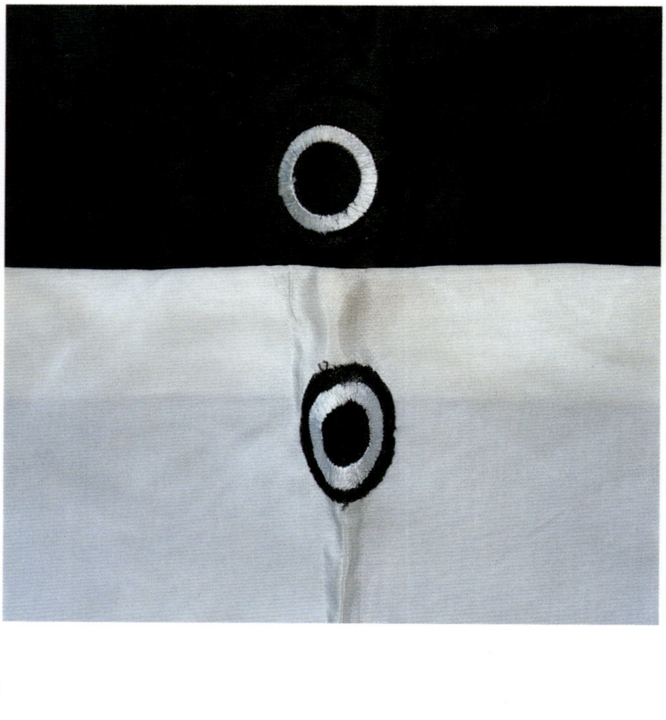

Fig. C2.1. World War I. Unidentified Medical Corps Lieutenant wearing a HE on felt or wool 2nd Corps patch.

Figs. C2.2 and C2.3. World War I. HE on wool.

Fig. C2.4. World War I. CS on satin applied to a wool base. Courtesy of US Army Military History Institute.

Fig. C2.5. World War I. ME on felt.

Figs. C2.7 and C2.8. World War I. Liberty Loan.

Fig. C2.6. World War I. A Signal Corps doughboy wearing a Liberty Loan style 2nd Corps patch.

Fig. C2.9. World War I. Unidentified Medical Corps doughboy wearing a 2nd Corps patch.

Figs. C2.10 and C2.11. World War I. Bullion on wool.

Fig. C2.12. World War I. Silk screen on thin cotton. Courtesy of US Army Military History Institute.

Fig. C2.13. World War I/Interwar. ME on felt.

Figs. C2.14 to C2.16. Interwar. ME on OD wool.

Fig. C2.17. Interwar. ME on blue wool.

Fig. C2.18. Interwar. 2nd Corps Cavalry. ME on wool applied to a yellow wool base. This type of patch is known to have been worn by the 104th Cavalry Regiment.

Fig. C2.19. Interwar. 2nd Corps Cavalry. ME on felt.

Fig. C2.20. Interwar/World War II. 2nd Corps Cavalry. FE

Fig. C2.21. Interwar/World War II. 2nd Corps Infantry. FE.

Fig. C2.22. Interwar. 2nd Corps Signal. ME on felt.

Fig. C2.23. World War II. 2nd Corps Signal. FE, ODB patch with machine added orange border.

Fig. C2.25. World War II. ME on twill.

Fig. C2.24. World War II. Major General Geoffrey, Commanding General of the 2nd Corps, congratulates Pfc. Emitering V. Lopez, conferring a medal for valor to Pfc. Emiter. Courtesy of US Army Military History Institute.

Figs. C2.26 and C2.27. World War II. FE, ODB.

Fig. C2.28. World War II. FE. Reversed variation featuring the Lion before the Eagle. It is unknown if this was intended to be worn on the right shoulder or simply a manufacturer's error.

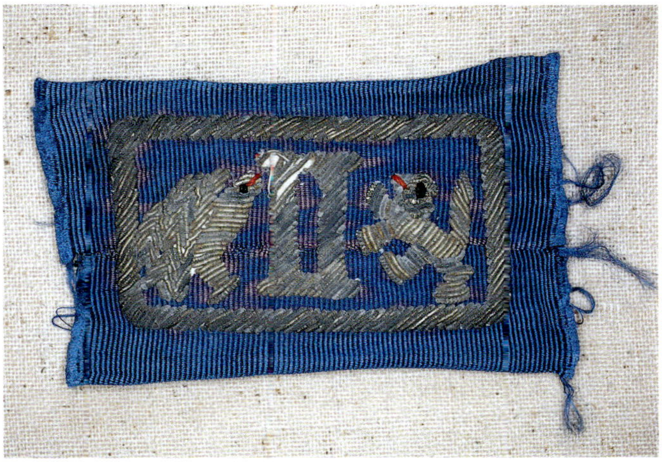

Fig. C2.29. World War II, Italy Bullion on ribbed satin.

Fig. C2.30. World War II, Italy. Bullion on satin applied to a wool base.

Fig. C2.31. World War II, Italy. Miniature patch type DI with spring pin closure.

Fig. C2.32. Post World War II, Germany. FE.

Fig. C3.1. World War I. Two unidentified doughboys; one from the 3rd Corps and the other from the 90th Division.

Figs. C3.2 to C3.4. World War I. Wool on wool.

Fig. C3.5. World War I. Cotton on velvet.

Fig. C3.6. World War I. ME on wool.

Fig. C3.7. World War I. ME on felt.

Fig. C3.9. World War I. Sgt. Bradley's (*see* p 108) bullion on wool 3rd Corps patch with added HE and bullion miniature Army of Occupation patch.

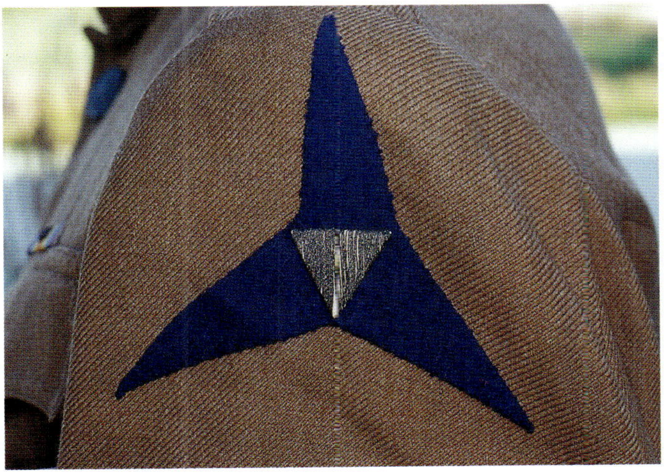

Figs. C3.10 and C3.11. World War I. Bullion on wool. These two examples were worn by Sergeant Arthur Coe of the 186th Aero Squadron.

Fig. C3.8. World War I. Sergeant Ben Bradley, 3rd Corps Artillery.

Figs. C3.12 and C3.13. Interwar. ME on wool.

Fig. C3.14. World War II. FE, ODB.

Fig. C3.15. World War II. FE blue border variation.

Fig. C4.1. World War I. Unidentified Infantry doughboy from the 4th Corps.

Fig. C4.2. World War I. Wool on wool.

Fig. C4.3. World War I. Wool on wool applied to an OD wool base.

Fig. C4.4. World War I. Felt with soutache detail and border.

Fig. C4.5. World War I. Felt on velvet applied to an OD wool base.

Fig. C4.7. World War I. All silk construction. This patch was worn by Craig Herbert of the 2nd Balloon Company.

Fig. C4.8. World War I/Interwar. Felt on felt.

Fig. C4.6. World War I. Unidentified 4th Corps doughboy.

Figs. C4.9. and C4.10. Interwar. ME on wool.

Fig. C4.11. World War II. FE.

Fig. C4.14. World War II. FE. Blue border variation.

Figs. C4.12 and C4.13. World War II. FE. Khaki border variation.

Fig. C4.15. World War II, Italy. Woven with ME border.

Fig. C5.1. World War I. Colonel George M. Russell, Assistant Chief of Staff, G-2, 5th Corps. During World War 1 the 5th Corps was another unit which utilized a variety of color variations to designate its different branches. The only variation not shown is for Engineers. That branch features two red triangles at the 4 and 8 O'clock positions.

Fig. C5.3. World War I. ME on felt.

Fig. C5.2. World War I. HE on wool.

Fig. C5.4. World War I. Liberty Loan.

Fig. C5.5. World War I. Unidentified 5th Corps Artilleryman. The image clearly shows the red section at the bottom of his patch denoting artillery.

Fig. C5.6. World War I. 5th Corps Artillery. Wool on wool.

Fig. C5.7. World War I. 5th Corps Artillery. All felt on wool.

Fig. C5.8. World War I. 5th Corps Artillery. Percy Eppehimer's HE on wool patch.

Fig. C5.11. World War I. 5th Corps Artillery. Liberty Loan.

Figs. C5.9 and C5.10. World War I. 5th Corps Artillery. ME on felt.

Fig. C5.12. World War I. 5th Corps Cavalry. Wool on wool.

Fig. C5.13. World War I. 5th Corps Cavalry. Liberty Loan. Although this is a 5th Corps Cavalry patch, this example was worn by PFC. Albert J. Kemnitzer of Company C, 317th Field Signal Battalion.

Fig. C5.14. World War I. 5th Corps Infantry. ME on felt. This patch was worn by PFC Nelson S. Miller, Headquarters Company, 52nd Pioneer Infantry.

Fig. C5.15. World War I. 5th Corps Infantry. Liberty Loan.

Fig. C5.16. World War I. 5th Corps Infantry. HE on wool with soutache borders. The significance of the one dark blue panel is unknown. It may represent a specific infantry unit assigned to the corps.

Fig. C5.17. World War I. 5th Corps Signals. Wool on wool.

Fig. C5.18. Interwar. ME on wool.

Fig. C5.19. Interwar. ME on wool. This reversed color variation is most likely a manufacturer's error.

Fig. C5.20. Interwar. ME on twill.

Fig. C5.21. Interwar. ME on wool.

Fig. C5.22. Interwar. ME on officer's dark OD wool elastique.

Fig. C5.23. Interwar/World War II. ME on felt.

Fig. C5.24. World War II. Technician 5th Grade Charles L. Webber shown with his invention of an air preheater. The device overcomes operational problems with generators used in low humidity areas. Tec. 5 Webber was with a Signal unit in the 5th Corps. U.S. Army Signal Corps.

Fig. C5.25. World War II. FE, ODB.

Fig. C5.26. Post World War II. US made FE patch with German made ME on felt tab.

Fig. C5.27. Post World War II, Germany. Woven.

Fig. C5.28. Post World War II, Germany. 5th Corps Artillery. FE.

Fig. C5.29. Post World War II, Germany. 5th Corps Artillery. Bullion on felt.

Fig. C6.1. World War I. Wool on wocl.

Fig. C6.2. World War I. HE on wool.

Fig. C6.3. World War I. Bullion on felt.

Fig. C6.4. World War I. Bullion on velvet.

Figs. C6.5 and C6.6. World War II. FE, ODB.

Fig. C6.7. Post World War II, Germany. FE.

Fig. C6.8. Post World War II, Germany. Bullion on felt with cord border.

Fig. C6.9. Post World War II, Japan. Bullion on felt.

Fig. C7.1. World War I. Unidentified 7th Corps doughboy.

Figs. C7.2 and C7.3. World War I. Wool on wool.

Fig. C7.4. World War I. Felt on felt.

Fig. C7.7. World War I. HE on wool. The dashed line is a cutting guide for the border shape of the patch.

Figs. C7.5 and C7.6. World War I. HE on wool.

Fig. C7.8. World War I. Quartermaster doughboy wearing a white border 7th Corps patch.

Fig. C7.9. World War I. CS on wool.

Figs. C7.10 to C7.12. World War I. Bullion on wool.

Fig. C7.13. World War I. Unidentified Cavalryman wearing a bullion on velvet 7th Corps patch. After the Armistice, Troops F and G of the 2nd Cavalry Regiment were assigned the 7th Corps.

Figs. C7.14 and C7.15. World War I. Bullion on velvet.

Fig. C7.16. World War I. Liberty Loan.

Fig. C7.20. Post World War II, Japan. HE quilted silk. This patch was one of a number of souvenir patches made for a nurse stationed in Japan after the war.

Figs. C7.17 to C7.19. World War II. FE, ODB.

Fig. C7.21. World War II. Private Frank J. Esposito, of the 50th Signal Bn., a message center dispatcher at the 7th Corps Headquarters, separates messages in Belgium, January 16, 1945. U.S. Army Signal Corps. On April 28, 1944 the second design 7th Corps patch using Roman numerals and a seven pointed star was approved, replacing the original shield and number design.

Fig. C7.22. World War II, Belgium. Twill applied to a wool base with HE numerals and ME border. The identification of the country of origin for this patch was made easy by the maker's label on the back.

Fig. C7.23. Post World War II, Germany. FE.

Fig. C7.24. Post World War II, Germany. Woven.

Fig. C7.25. World War II/Post World War II. US made FE patch with German added bullion.

Fig. C7.27. Post World War II, Germany. HE on wool with bullion details and bullion cord border.

Fig. C7.26. Post World War II, Germany. FE patch with added bullion.

Fig. C7.28. Post World War II, Germany. HE and bullion numeral on a velvet star applied to a wool base with bullion details and border.

Figs. C7.29 and C7.30. Post World War II. Embroidered on felt patch stickers, unknown use.

Fig. C8.1. World War II. Technical Sergeant Walter Frank.

Fig. C8.2. World War I. HE on wool.

Fig. C8.3. World War I. ME on wool.

Fig. C8.4. Interwar/World War II. ME on felt.

Fig. C8.5. World War II. ME on twill.

Fig. C8.6. World War II. ME on twill. In this variation the outer blue border touches the inner white border.

Fig. C8.7. World War II. FE, ODB.

Fig. C8.8. Post World War II, Germany. Bullion on felt.

Figs. C9.1 and C9.2. World War I. Wool on wool.

Fig. C9.3. World War I/Interwar. Felt on felt.

Fig. C9.4. World War I. Liberty Loan.

Figs. C9.5 and C9.6. Interwar. Felt on felt.

Fig. C9.7. Interwar. Felt on felt on a wool base.

Fig. C9.8. World War II. Comparison of two different US made FE, ODB patches.

Fig. C9.9. World War II. FE.

Fig. C9.10. Post World War II. US made FE patch with added bullion.

Fig. C9.11. Post World War II, Germany. FE.

Fig. C9.14. Post World War II, Japan. FE. The design of the patch is embroidered through a woven background.

Figs. C9.12 and C9.13. Post World War II, Japan. FE.

Fig. C9.15. Post World War II, Japan. HE silk on silk.

Fig. C9.16. Post World War II, Japan. All silk fully HE with a quilted background.

Figs. C9.17 to C9.19. Post World War II, Japan. Felt on felt with bullion details.

Fig. C9.20. Post World War II, Japan. HE on felt with bullion details.

Fig. C9.21. Post World War II, Japan. HE silk with quilted background and bullion detail.

Fig. C9.22. Post World War II, Japan. Red bullion on felt.

Fig. C9.23. Post World War II, Korea. ME on twill.

Fig. C10.1. World War II. FE.

Fig. C10.2. World War II. FE. This variation lacks the cross bars for the top and bottom of the Roman numeral.

Fig. C10.3. World War II. FE. Blue border variation.

Fig. C10.6. Post World War II, Germany. FE.

Figs. C10.4 and C10.5. World War II/Post World War II. Front and back of an unusual FE patch.

Fig. C10.7. Post World War II, Germany. HE on felt

Figs. C10.8 and C10.9. Post World War II, Japan. Fully hand embroidered silk. While under his command during the Korean War, Major General Edward M. Almond ordered that the 10th Corps patch be worn with the white field up, opposite of how it was worn during World War II and counter to official regulations.

Figs. C10.10 to C10.12. Post World War II, Japan. Bullion on felt.

Fig. C11.1. World War II. 1st design 11th Corps. FE.

Fig. C11.2. World War II. 1st design 11th Corps. Blue border variation FE.

Fig. C11.3. World War II. 2nd design 11th Corps. FE.

Fig. C11.4. Post World War II, Japan. 2nd design 11th Corps. Fully hand embroidered silk.

Fig. C12.1. Interwar. Felt on felt.

Fig. C12.2. World War II. FE, ODB.

Figs. C12.3 and C12.4. World War II, England. FE.

Figs. C12.5 and C12.6. World War II/Post World War II, TM. ME on twill.

Fig. C12.7. Post World War II, Germany. FE. Red windmill variation.

Fig. C12.8. Post World War II, Germany. Bullion on felt with bullion cord border.

Fig. C13.1. World War II. FE. These two examples have left and right facing clover leaf stems.

Fig. C13.3. Post World War II, Germany. HE on wool with bullion detail and border.

Fig. C13.2. Post World War II, Germany. Satin triangle on a velvet clover leaf applied to a wool base with a ME border.

Fig. C14.1. World War II. FE.

Fig. C14.2. Post World War II, Germany. FE.

Fig. C15.1. World War II. 1st design 15th Corps patch. FE.

Fig. C15.2. World War II. 2nd design 15th Corps patch. FE.

Fig. C16.1. Post World War II. Colonel Cecil W. Nist, Chief of Staff, 16th Corps, at center, in his office at Camp Sendai, Japan with Colonel Francis E. Conder, Corps Special Service Officer and librarian Lynn Delaune. Courtesy of US Army Military History Institute.

Fig. C16.2. World War II. FE, ODB.

Fig. C16.3. Post World War II, Germany. FE. Courtesy of US Army Military History Institute.

Fig. C16.4. Post World War II, Japan. FE silk.

Fig. C16.5. Post World War II, Japan. Felt and bullion on wool.

Fig. C18.1. Post World War II. An unidentified Lieutenant Colonel wearing a 18th Airborne Corps patch on his right shoulder. Courtesy of US Army Military History Institute. The 18th Corps was redesignated the 18th Airborne Corps on August 27, 1944. When worn as a Corps patch it was worn in a diamond pattern with the dragon facing out to the left. When worn in Airborne configuration normally the patch is square with the dragon facing down. It has been reported that occasionally it was worn as shown in Fig C18.7.

Fig. C18.2. World War II. ME on twill.

Fig. C18.3. World War II, England. ME.

Fig. C18.4. Post World War II, Germany. FE.

Fig. C18.5. World War II/Post World War II. Comparison of the backs of the two previous examples with the English made example on the left and German made on the right.

Fig. C18.6. Post World War II, Germany. ME and ME bullion on velvet. This example is still in the original cellophane wrapper.

Fig. C18.7. Post World War II, Japan. Bullion on felt.

Fig. C18.8. World War II/Post WWII. Felt on felt jacket back patch. This alternate design was supposedly used by the artillery elements of the 18th Airborne Corps.

Fig. C19.1. World War II. Staff Sergeant Robert A. French and Technician 4th Class Dody A. Wilson entering a circus playing in Friedberg, Germany on July 24, 1945. Sgt. French is wearing a ME on felt 3rd design 19th Corps patch. An interesting note is the angle the patch is being worn; the tomahawk is angled forward rather than being vertical. This method of wear has been observed on other period uniforms. U.S. Army Signal Corps.

Fig. C.19.2. World War II. 1st Design 19th Corps. FE.

Fig. C19 3. World War II. 2nd Design 19th Corps. FE.

Fig. C19.4. World War II. 3rd Design 19th Corps. FE.

Fig. C19.5. World War II. 3rd Design 19th Corps. ME on felt.

Fig. C19.6. World War II. 3rd Design 19th Corps. ME on wool.

Fig. C19.7. Post World War II, Germany. 3rd Design 19th Corps. Miniature patch. HE and bullion on felt with bullion cord border.

Fig. C20.01 World War II. ME on twill.

Fig. C20.2. World War II. FE.

Fig. C20.3. Post World War II, Japan. FE. Black background variation.

Fig. C20.4. Post World War II, Japan. HE silk background and bullion.

Fig. C20.6. Post World War II. 20th Corps Pistol Team patch. CS on felt.

Fig. C20.5. Post World War II. 20th Corps Pistol Team patch. US made FE patch applied to a felt background with CS lettering and border.

Fig. C21.1. Post World War II. Mr. Franklin P Adams of the USO show "Information Please" talks with Technician 4th Grade Alex Cozak and Pfc. John V. Liptak before a show in Gmund, Germany, July 15, 1945. U.S Army Signal Corps.

Fig. C21.2. World War II. ME on twill.

Fig. C21.3. World War II. FE.

Fig. C21.4. Post World War II, Germany. HE and bullion on wool applied to an OD wool background.

Fig. C22.1. Post World War II. Major General Ernest N. Harmon, Commanding General of the 22nd Corps, presenting a diploma for a counter intelligence course at an US Army school in Munchen-Gladbach, Germany, May 11, 1945. U.S. Army Signal Corps.

Fig. C22.2. World War II. FE.

Fig. C22.3. Post World War II, Germany. FE.

Fig. C22.4. Post World War II, Germany. Bullion on felt.

Fig. C23.1. World War II. ME on twill.

Fig. C23.2. World War II. FE.

Fig. C23.3. Post World War II, Germany. HE and bullion on felt with a cord border.

Fig. C23.4. Post World War II, Germany. Bullion on wool and HE on bullion fabric background with a bullion border.

Fig. C24.1. Post World War II. Staff Sergeant Edward M. Broderick of the 556th MAMB Company receives a Drivers Medal from Captain H. H. Dills in Seoul, Korea, April 19, 1948. Courtesy of US Army Military History Institute.

Fig. C24.2. Post World War II. Sergeant William R. Smithdale's US made FE patch and Japanese made bullion on silk miniature Garrison Cap patch.

Fig. C24.3. World War II, Australia. ME on felt.

Fig. C24.4. Post World War II, Korea. HE silk.

Fig. C24.5. Post World War II, Japan. Bullion on velvet.

Fig. C24.6. Post World War II, Germany. FE.

Fig. C24.7. Post World War II. US made FE patch with German added bullion

Fig. C36.1. World War II. FE.

Fig. C36.2. World War II. Fully embroidered in yellow.

Bibliography

Britton, Jack and George Washington Jr. *U.S. Military Shoulder Patches of the United States Armed Forces.* Tulsa, Oklahoma: M.C.N. Press, 1985.

Davis, Brian L. *US Army Cloth Insignia 1941 to the Present.* Dorest, England: Arms and Armour Press Ltd., 1987.

Department of the Army. *The Army Lineage Book Volume II: Infantry.* Washington: U.S. Government Printing Office, 1953.

Diver, Thomas R., ed. *Shoulder Sleeve Insignia: Insignia of Rank, Service Ribbons, Decorations and Insignia of the U. S. Armed Forces.* Baltimore, Maryland: Reese Press, n.d.

Emerson, William K. *Encyclopedia of United States Army Insignia and Uniforms.* Norman: University of Oklahoma Press, 1996.

Forty, George. *US Army Handbook 1939-1945.* United Kingdom: Alan Sutton Publishing Ltd., 1995.

Historical Section Army War College. *Order of Battle of the United States Land Forces In The World War American Expeditionary Forces.* Washington, D.C.: United States Government Printing Office Washington, 1937.

Lewis, Kenneth. *Doughboy to GI US Army Clothing and Equipment 1900-1945.* West Midlands, England: Norman D. Landing Publishing, 1993.

Morgan, George O. and Mark Warren. *Shoulder Sleeve Insignia of the A.E.F. 1917-1919.* Keokuk, Iowa: Hill Printing Co., 1986.

Petersen, Gordon A. J. *A Guide to U. S. Army Insignia and Decorations* Racine, Wisconsin: Whitman Publishing Co., 1941.

Rottman, Gordon. *U.S. Army Airborne 1940-90.* London, England: Osprey Publishing Ltd., 1990.

Smith and Pelz. *Shoulder Sleeve Insignia of the U.S. Armed Forces 1941-1945.* N.p., 1981.

Stanton, Shelby. *U.S. Army Uniforms of The Korean War.* Harrisburg, Pennsylvania: Stackpole Books, 1992.

Stanton, Shelby. *U.S. Army Uniforms of World War 2.* Harrisburg, Pennsylvania: Stackpole Books, 1991.

Stanton, Shelby L. *World War 2 Order of Battle.* New York, New York: Galahad Books, 1984.

Stringer, Harry R. *Heroes All!* Washington, D.C.: Fasset Publishing Co., 1919.

UNITED STATES NAVY PATCHES SERIES

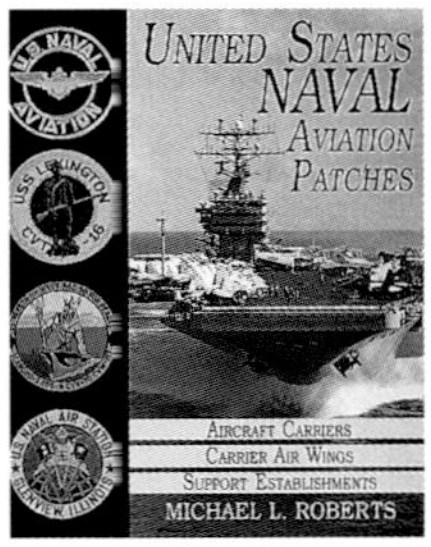

Volume I:
Aircraft Carriers/Carrier Air Wings/Support Establishments
Size: 8 1/2" x 11" ■ over 1,000 patches ■ 160 pp.
ISBN: 0-88740-753-6 ■ hard cover ■ $29.95

Volume II:
Aircraft/Attack Squadrons/Helicopter Squadrons
Size: 8 1/2" x 11" ■ over 1,000 patches in color ■ 144 pp.
ISBN: 0-88740-801-X ■ hard cover ■ $29.95

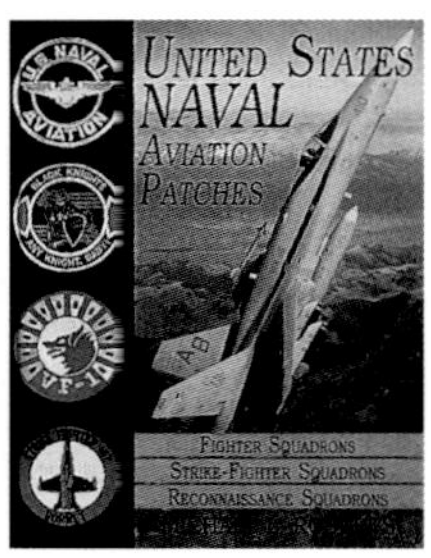

Volume III:
Fighter/Fighter Attack/Recon. Squadrons
Size: 8 1/2" x 11" ■ over 1,000 patches in color ■ 168 pp.
ISBN: 0-88740-802-8 ■ hard cover ■ $29.95

Volume IV:
Amphibious Forces/SEAL Teams/Fleets/Flotillas/Groups
Size: 8 1/2" x 11" ■ over 1,000 patches in color ■ 168 pp.
ISBN: 0-7643-0068-7 ■ hard cover ■ $29.95

Volume V: SHIPS:
Battleships/Cruisers/Destroyers/LSTs/Etc.
Size: 8 1/2" x 11" ■ 1,660+ patches in full color ■ 208 pp.
ISBN: 0-7643-0144-6 ■ hard cover ■ $39.95

Volume VI:
Submarines
Size: 8 1/2" x 11" ■ over 650 patches in full color ■ 76 pp.
ISBN: 0-7643-0186-1 ■ hard cover ■ $35.00